Scott Foresman

Kindergarten Unit Benchmark Assessments
Teacher's Manual

Reading STREET

Grade K

PEARSON
Scott Foresman

Editorial Offices: Glenview, Illinois • Parsippany, New Jersey • New York, New York
Sales Offices: Boston, Massachusetts • Duluth, Georgia • Glenview, Illinois
Coppell, Texas • Sacramento, California • Mesa, Arizona

ISBN: 0-328-19668-1

Copyright © Pearson Education, Inc.

11 12 13 14 15 16 17 18 19 20 V036 15 14 13 12 11 10

Contents

OVERVIEW

Scott Foresman Reading Street provides a wide array of group-administered formal tests and classroom assessments to support instruction. This Teacher's Manual provides information and directions for administering and scoring the Kindergarten Unit Benchmark Assessments and blackline assessment pages that may be copied and used with children in the classroom. Consumable Kindergarten Unit Benchmark Assessment booklets are also available.

There are six Kindergarten Unit Benchmark Assessments, one for each of the six units. The content of these tests is based on targeted skills taught in each unit in these different areas:

Comprehension	Writing
Phonemic Awareness	Word Knowledge
Phonics	Word Reading

The primary purpose of the Kindergarten Unit Benchmark Assessments is to help you collect information about individual children's reading, writing, and language skills development. This information can be used to make instructional decisions about each child, identify specific strengths and weaknesses, and assess children's progress throughout the year.

USING THESE ASSESSMENTS

The Kindergarten Unit Benchmark Assessments are designed to be administered at the end of each unit. Assessment tasks can be given to individuals, small groups, or the whole class—depending on the nature of each activity.

Since children will be more capable or less capable of handling these assessments at different times, teachers should use their own professional judgment in determining when to conduct assessments and how many parts of the assessments to administer.

Later sections of this Teacher's Manual provide guidelines and directions for administering and scoring each Unit Benchmark Assessment. Each task in the Unit Benchmark Assessment is designed to be administered in one sitting. You may administer more than one task in a sitting. If a child cannot manage a given task, you may move on to a different task or discontinue the assessment at that point.

SCORING THE ASSESSMENTS

For each task in the Unit Benchmark Assessments, the directions include guidelines for scoring and evaluating each child's performance. Each assessment is designed to be scored by skill, and the results are based on a 3-point rating scale. Points on the scale can generally be defined as follows:

Proficient (+) The child answers all questions correctly; additional practice should be challenging.

Developing (✓) The child answers most questions correctly; additional practice should be guided.

Emerging (–) The child answers few questions correctly, showing signs of beginning to understand the skill; additional practice should be targeted.

In a Phonics activity, for example, a child who answers 5 out of 5 questions correctly would receive a "Proficient" rating. A child who answers 3 or 4 of the 5 questions correctly would receive a "Developing" rating. Children who answer fewer than 3 questions correctly would be rated "Emerging." Specific criteria for all three ratings are provided with each assessment task.

At the end of the directions for each unit, you will find an evaluation chart that may be copied for classroom use. The **Individual Record** for each unit may be used to record the results of the Unit Benchmark Assessments for each child. At the back of this Teacher's Manual, you will find a Class Record chart. The **Class Record** (T73) may be used to record results on any Unit Benchmark Assessment for all children in the class. Both of these charts will assist you in determining instructional needs for the children in your class.

INTERPRETING RESULTS

Each Unit Benchmark Assessment measures different skills. Since every assessed skill may be considered essential to the child's progress in later units, a child's performance should be evaluated on the basis of each skill. However, the following guidelines may help to interpret a child's performance on all the skills assessed in each unit:

- A child who receives a "Proficient" rating on all or most of the tasks in a unit is likely to need additional challenges in the course of instruction.

- A child who receives a "Developing" rating on most of the tasks in a unit will most likely benefit from guided instruction in the next unit.

- A child who receives an "Emerging" rating on three or more skills in a unit may need targeted instruction in specific concepts and skills.

Specific criteria for interpreting results in each task are provided in later sections of this Teacher's Manual.

DIRECTIONS FOR ADMINISTERING
UNIT BENCHMARK ASSESSMENTS

This section of the Manual provides directions for administering each Unit Benchmark Assessment for Units 1–6. Directions for each unit begin on the pages listed.

Unit 1 – T8
Unit 2 – T18
Unit 3 – T28
Unit 4 – T38
Unit 5 – T50
Unit 6 – T63

Each Unit Benchmark Assessment has different tasks. The directions for each task indicate whether it is designed for administration to an individual, a small group, or the whole class. In many cases, you will be able to choose from two or three of these options in planning how to administer each assessment.

The tasks in these assessments have corresponding pages for children to use in responding to questions. For each task, you will see a reproduction of the test page in the directions (with correct responses indicated, if applicable).

At the end of the directions for each unit, you will find the **Individual Record** for that unit. You may want to make a copy of the Individual Record for each child and a copy of the **Class Record** (T73) for the whole class to help you record and evaluate the results of each assessment.

Each task in the Unit Benchmark Assessment is designed to be administered in one sitting of 5 to 10 minutes. You may administer more than one task in a sitting. If a child cannot manage a given task, you may move on to a different task or discontinue the assessment at that point.

In the pages that follow, directions printed in **bold** type are intended to be read aloud. Text printed in regular type provides information for your use only.

UNIT 1 DIRECTIONS

1. Letter Naming
(Individual)

Purpose: Assesses ability to recognize uppercase and lowercase letters of the alphabet.

Directions in **bold** are to be read aloud; others are for your information only.

Hand out student page 2. You will ask the child to say the names of the letters as you point to them. Move across the lines from left to right as you point to the letters so the child is asked to identify the letters in random order. For some children, it may be necessary to administer the assessment in two sessions. (Note: You may want to make a copy of the page for each child to record his or her performance.)

I will point to a letter and you will tell me the name of that letter.

Scoring: For each child, count the total number of letters correctly named. Using the guidelines below, record each child's score on the Individual Record for the Unit 1 Benchmark Assessment (T17).

Number Correct	Rating	
All	Proficient	+
45 – 51	Developing	✓
Less than 45	Emerging	–

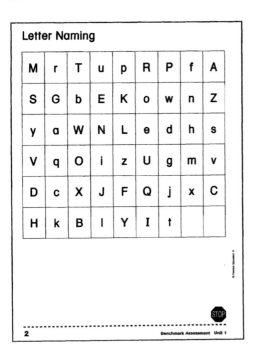

Letter Naming								
M	r	T	u	p	R	P	f	A
S	G	b	E	K	o	w	n	Z
y	a	W	N	L	e	d	h	s
V	q	O	i	z	U	g	m	v
D	c	X	J	F	Q	j	x	C
H	k	B	l	Y	I	t		

2   Benchmark Assessment Unit 1

2. Phonological Awareness: Rhyming

(Individual or small group)

Purpose: Assesses ability to recognize rhyme.

Hand out student page 3. Use the following directions to administer the assessment, beginning with the sample question. Children are to respond by circling the answer to each question. If children are unfamiliar with circling answers, write three words in a row on the chalkboard and demonstrate how to draw a circle around one of the words.

Now I want you to listen for rhyming words. Let's do the first one together. Find the small star at the top of the page. Put your finger on it. Now look at the picture by the star. It is a *boat*. Say the word. (boat) Look at the three pictures in the same row: *cat, coat, boy*. Which word rhymes with *boat—cat, coat, or boy*? (Pause.) Yes, *coat* rhymes with *boat*. Draw a circle around the picture of the *coat* because *coat* is the word that rhymes with *boat*.

When you are sure that each child understands the task and has followed the directions for completing the sample item, administer each test item.

1. **Now move down to the next row where you see the square. Put your finger on it. Look at the picture by the square. It is a *rake*. Look at the three pictures in the same row: *sock, rug, cake*. Draw a circle around the word that rhymes with *rake . . . rake*.**

2. **Move down to the next row, the circle, where you see the *dish*. Look at the pictures: *desk, fish, brush*. Draw a circle around the word that rhymes with *dish . . . dish*.**

3. **Move down to the next row, the triangle, where you see the *clock*. Look at the pictures: *duck, clown, rock*. Draw a circle around the word that rhymes with *clock . . . clock*.**

4. **Move down to the last row, the heart, where you see the *bone*. Look at the pictures: *phone, bean, mouse*. Draw a circle around the word that rhymes with *bone . . . bone*.**

Scoring: For each child, mark the answer to each question correct or incorrect. Then count the total number correct for each child. Using the guidelines below, record the child's score on the Individual Record for the Unit 1 Benchmark Assessment (T17).

Number Correct	Rating	
4	Proficient	+
3	Developing	✓
Less than 3	Emerging	–

3. Word Knowledge: High-Frequency Words

(Individual or small group)

Purpose: Assesses ability to recognize high-frequency words.

Hand out student page 4. Use the following directions to administer the assessment. If necessary, demonstrate on the chalkboard how to draw a line from the picture to the word.

Let's find some words you know.

Find the picture of the star. Put your finger on it. Now look at the words on the page. Find the word *little*. Draw a line from the star to the word *little*.

Move down to the picture of the bird. Put your finger on it. Now find the word *I*. Draw a line from the bird to the word *I*.

Move down to the picture of the dog. Put your finger on it. Now find the word *to*. Draw a line from the dog to the word *to*.

Move down to the picture of the fish. Put your finger on it. Now find the word *am*. Draw a line from the fish to the word *am*.

Move down to the picture of the cat. Put your finger on it. Now find the word *the*. Draw a line from the cat to the word *the*.

Move down to the picture of the horse. Put your finger on it. Now find the word *a*. Draw a line from the horse to the word *a*.

Scoring: For each child, count the total number of words matched correctly. Using the guidelines below, record the child's score on the Individual Record for the Unit 1 Benchmark Assessment (T17).

Number Correct	Rating	
6	Proficient	+
4 – 5	Developing	✓
Less than 4	Emerging	–

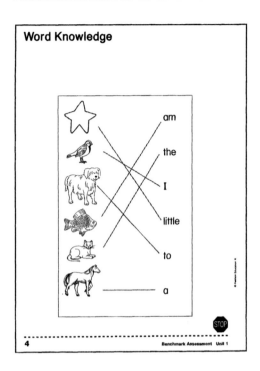

4. Listening Comprehension: Character

(Individual or small group)

Purpose: Assesses general comprehension.

Hand out student page 5. Read the story aloud. Then read each question that follows. Children are to respond by circling the answer to each question. If children are unfamiliar with circling answers, draw three simple pictures in a row on the chalkboard and demonstrate how to draw a circle around one of the pictures.

I am going to read a story about a girl named Maria. Then I will ask you some questions. Listen carefully. Here is the story.

Everyone in Maria's family loved to sing. They sang all the time. Maria's mom sang while she cooked dinner. Her dad sang while he washed the dishes. And her sister sang while she swept the floor. Maria sang too, but only when no one could hear her. She thought she did not sing well.

"Maria, sing with us," begged her dad every night after dinner. He started to sing her favorite song. Everyone joined in—except Maria.

But later, when Maria was alone in her bedroom, she did what she did every night. She sat by her window and sang. Her voice drifted out into the warm night air.

The next morning as Maria walked past the house next door, she heard someone singing her favorite song. Just then her neighbor Mr. Suarez opened the door and came outside.

"It's a beautiful day, isn't it?" he said to Maria.

"Yes it is," Maria answered. "But the day is not as beautiful as the voice that I hear coming from your house. Who is that singing?"

"That's my pet parrot," said Mr. Suarez.

"Your parrot," said Maria in surprise. "But how did your parrot learn to sing that song.

"He learned it from you," answered Mr. Suarez. "We listen to you sing every night. He is singing in your voice. You're the one with the beautiful voice."

That night Maria finally sang along with her family.

Now I am going to ask you some questions about the story. For each question that I ask, there are three pictures. Draw a circle around the picture that shows the best answer. Listen carefully.

1. Look at the first row of pictures at the top of the page where you see the square. Put your finger on the square. What did Maria's family like to do? *Eat dinner . . . sing songs . . . or read books?* Draw a circle around the picture that shows the best answer.

2. Move down to the next row of pictures where you see the circle. Put your finger on the circle. How did Maria feel about her singing at the beginning of the story? *Bad . . . proud . . . or scared?* Draw a circle around the picture that shows how she felt about her singing at the beginning of the story.

3. Move down to the next row of pictures where you see the triangle. Put your finger on the triangle. Where did Maria sing? *In her bedroom . . . at breakfast . . . or in school?* Draw a circle around the picture that shows where Maria sang at night.

4. Move down to the next row of pictures where you see the heart. Put your finger on the heart. Who heard Maria singing every night? *Her parents . . . her friends . . . or Mr. Suarez?* Draw a circle around the picture that shows who heard Maria singing every night.

5. Move down to the next row of pictures where you see the rectangle. Put your finger on the rectangle. How did Maria feel when she found out that a parrot was singing? *Sad . . . surprised . . . or mad?* Draw a circle around the picture that shows how she felt.

Scoring: For each child, mark the answer to each question correct or incorrect. Then count the total number correct for each child. Using the guidelines below, record the child's score on the Individual Record for the Unit 1 Benchmark Assessment (T17).

Number Correct	Rating	
5	Proficient	+
3 – 4	Developing	✓
Less than 3	Emerging	–

5. Writing: Picture of Self and Writing Own Name

(Individual, small group, or whole class)

Purpose: Assesses ability of child to draw self and write name.

Hand out student page 6. Instruct children as follows.

Now we are going to do something different. Look at the picture frame on your page. Draw a picture of yourself in the picture frame. Be sure to include details in your picture. Then write your name on the line under the picture frame.

Scoring: After children complete their work, place a checkmark beside each attribute the child has included in the drawing and the writing. Using the guidelines below, evaluate the child's work and record the child's score on the Individual Record for the Unit 1 Benchmark Assessment (T17).

Scoring Guidelines	Rating	
Draws a detailed picture and writes name correctly. Includes many attributes.	Proficient	+
Draws a recognizable picture and writes some letters of name correctly. Includes some attributes.	Developing	✓
Attempts to draw a picture and write name, but both are less than complete and correct. Includes few attributes.	Emerging	–

Writing

Attributes

Picture: ___ eyes ___ nose ___ mouth ___ hair
___ neck ___ body ___ clothes ___ arms
___ hands ___ legs ___ feet

Name: ___ all letters are present ___ all letters are written correctly
___ first letter is capitalized

STOP

6   Benchmark Assessment Unit 1

INDIVIDUAL RECORD

Unit 1 Benchmark Assessment

Child's Name _____ Date _____

Directions: Record the results of the Unit 1 Benchmark Assessment by marking Proficient (+), Developing (✓), or Emerging (–) beside each assessed skill.

Unit 1 Assessed Skills	Proficient (+)	Developing (✓)	Emerging (–)
Letter Naming			
Phonological Awareness: Rhyming			
Word Knowledge: High-Frequency Words			
Listening Comprehension: Character			
Writing: Picture of Self and Writing Own Name			

Notes/Observations

UNIT 2 DIRECTIONS

1. Phonemic Awareness: Initial Sounds (/m/, /t/, short a, /s/, /p/, /k/ spelled c, short i)
(Individual or small group)

Purpose: Assesses ability to recognize initial sounds.

Directions in **bold** are to be read aloud; others are for your information only.

Hand out student pages 2 and 3. Use the following directions to administer the test, beginning with the sample question.

We are going to listen for the beginning sound in a word. Listen carefully. Let's do the first one together. Find the small star at the top of the page. Put your finger on it. Now look at the three pictures in the row beside the star: *pot, fan, pencil.* **Listen to the beginning sound of each word:** *pot, fan, pencil.* **Two of the words begin with the same sound. One of the words begins with a different sound. Which two words have the same beginning sound?** (Pause.) **Yes,** *pot* **and** *pencil* **have the same beginning sound. Draw a circle around the pictures of the** *pot* **and the** *pencil* **because they begin with the same sound.**

When you are sure that each child understands the task and has followed the directions for completing the sample item, administer each test item.

1. **Move down to the next row where you see the square. Put your finger on the square. Look at the three pictures in the same row:** *moon, mop, house.* **Draw a circle around the two pictures that have the same sound at the beginning:** *moon . . . mop . . . house.*

2. **Move down to the next row where you see the circle. Put your finger on the circle. Look at the pictures:** *ball, table, tire.* **Draw a circle around the two pictures that have the same sound at the beginning:** *ball . . . table . . . tire.*

3. **Move down to the next row where you see the triangle. Put your finger on the triangle. Look at the pictures:** *apple, umbrella, ant.* **Draw a circle around the two pictures that have the same beginning sound:** *apple . . . umbrella . . . ant.*

4. **Move down to the next row where you see the heart. Put your finger on the heart. Look at the pictures in the row:** *sun, soap, cake.* **Draw a circle around the two pictures that have the same beginning sound:** *sun . . . soap . . . cake.*

5. **Now look at the next page. Go to the first row where you see the square. Put your finger on the square. Look at the pictures in the row:** *rake, pig, pond.* **Draw a circle around the two pictures that have the same beginning sound:** *rake . . . pig . . . pond.*

© Pearson Education K

6. **Move down to the next row where you see the circle. Put your finger on the circle. Look at the pictures in the row:** *cat, foot, cup.* **Draw a circle around the two pictures that have the same beginning sound:** *cat . . . foot . . . cup.*

7. **Move down to the last row where you see the triangle. Put your finger on the triangle. Look at the pictures in the row:** *igloo, inch, octopus.* **Draw a circle around the two pictures that have the same beginning sound:** *igloo . . . inch . . . octopus.*

Scoring: For each child, mark the answer to each question correct or incorrect. Then count the total number correct for each child. Using the guidelines below, record the child's score on the Individual Record for the Unit 2 Benchmark Assessment (T27).

Number Correct	Rating	
7	Proficient	+
5 – 6	Developing	✓
Less than 5	Emerging	–

2. Phonics: Letter-Sound Correspondence (m, t, short a, s, p, c, short i)

(Individual or small group)

Purpose: Assesses ability to connect sound to letter.

Hand out student pages 4 and 5. Use the following directions to administer the assessment, beginning with the sample question.

Now we are going to find the letter for a sound. Let's do the first one together. Find the small star at the top of the page. Put your finger on it. Now look at the picture by the star. It is a *pin*. The middle sound in *pin* is /i/. Now look at the letters in the row next to the picture. Which is the letter for /i/? (Pause.) **Yes, the last letter in the row is the letter for /i/. Draw a circle around the letter for /i/.**

When you are sure that each child understands the task and has followed the directions for completing the sample item, administer each test item.

1. **Move down to the next row where you see the square. Put your finger on the square. Look at the picture of the *map* by the square. The first sound in *map* is /m/. Now look at the letters in the row next to the picture. What is the letter for /m/? Circle the letter for /m/.**

2. **Move down to the next row where you see the circle. Put your finger on the circle. Look at the picture of the *top* by the circle. The first sound in *top* is /t/. What is the letter for /t/? Circle the letter for /t/.**

3. **Move down to the next row where you see the triangle. Put your finger on the triangle. Look at the picture of the *mat* by the triangle. The middle sound in *mat* is /a/. What is the letter for /a/? Circle the letter for /a/.**

4. **Move down to the next row where you see the heart. Put your finger on the heart. Look at the picture of the *sock* by the heart. The first sound in *sock* is /s/. What is the letter for /s/? Circle the letter for /s/.**

5. **Now look at the next page. Go to the first row where you see the square. Put your finger on the square. Look at the picture of the *pan* by the square. The first sound in *pan* is /p/. What is the letter for /p/? Circle the letter for /p/.**

6. **Move down to the next row where you see the circle. Put your finger on the circle. Look at the picture of the *car* by the circle. The first sound in *car* is /k/. What is the letter for /k/? Circle the letter for /k/.**

7. **Move down to the last row where you see the triangle. Put your finger on the triangle. Look at the picture of the *fin* of the fish by the triangle. The middle sound in *fin* is /i/. What is the letter for /i/? Circle the letter for /i/.**

Scoring: For each child, mark the answer to each question correct or incorrect. Then count the total number correct for each child. Using the guidelines below, record the child's score on the Individual Record for the Unit 2 Benchmark Assessment (T27).

Number Correct	Rating	
7	Proficient	+
5 – 6	Developing	✓
Less than 5	Emerging	–

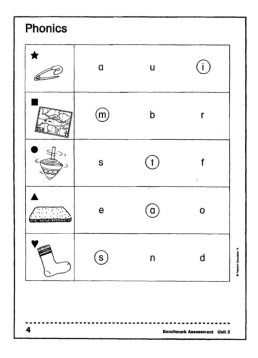

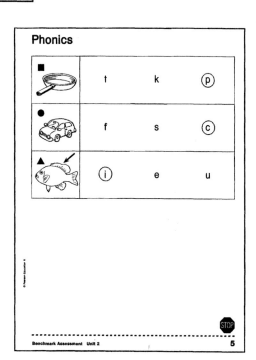

© Pearson Education K

3. Word Knowledge: High-Frequency Words

(Individual or small group)

Purpose: Assesses ability to recognize high-frequency words.

Hand out student page 6. As you say a word aloud, the child will circle it. Move through the assessment quickly to make sure you are assessing the child's ability to recognize the high-frequency words quickly.

1. Now I am going to say one word in each row, and you are going to circle the word that I am saying. Find the star and put your finger on it. Now look at the three words in that row. Draw a circle around the word *have ... have.*

2. Move down to the next row. Find the square and put your finger on it. Look at the three words. Circle the word *is ... is.*

3. Move down to the next row. Find the circle and put your finger on it. Look at the three words. Circle the word *we ... we.*

4. Move down to the next row. Find the triangle and put your finger on it. Look at the three words. Circle the word *my ... my.*

5. Move down to the next row. Find the heart and put your finger on it. Look at the three words. Circle the word *like ... like.*

6. Move down to the next row. Find the rectangle and put your finger on it. Look at the 3 words. Circle the word *he ... he.*

7. Move down to the next row. Find the diamond and put your finger on it. Look at the three words. Circle the word *for ... for.*

Scoring: For each child, mark the answer to each question correct or incorrect. Then count the total number of words circled correctly. Using the guidelines below, record the child's score on the Individual Record for the Unit 2 Benchmark Assessment (T27).

Number Correct	Rating	
7	Proficient	+
5 – 6	Developing	✓
Less than 5	Emerging	–

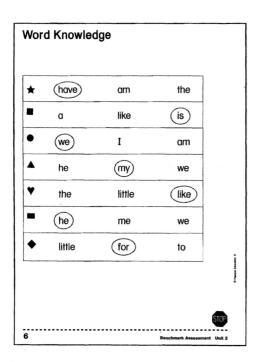

4. Listening Comprehension: Setting

(Individual, small group, or whole class)

Purpose: Assesses general comprehension.

Hand out student page 7. Read the story aloud. Then read each question that follows. Children will circle the answer to each question. Pause after each question to allow time for the children to mark their answers.

Now I am going to read a story about a boy named Michael. Then I will ask you some questions. Listen carefully. Here is the story.

Michael turned on the radio. He wanted to hear the weather report.

"You don't need the weatherman," said his father. "Just look outside."

Michael looked out the window. Everything was covered with snow, and it was still snowing.

Michael sighed. Now he wouldn't be able to go to his friend Peter's house to spend the night. The heavy snow was making it dangerous to drive.

"We can walk to Peter's house in about 20 minutes even in this snow," said Michael's father. "We can use your sled to carry your stuff. Let's go!"

Michael hurried to get his backpack. Then he and his father put on their winter jackets, hats, boots, and gloves. They tied Michael's backpack to the sled and dragged the sled out of the garage.

The streets were silent. Even though it was nighttime, everything looked bright because of the snow. Michael and his father walked quietly. They took turns pulling the sled.

Twenty minutes later they arrived at Peter's house and knocked at the door. Peter started to laugh as soon as he opened the door. "You two look like snowmen," he said.

"Then we won't have to build one," Michael said.

But of course the boys did build a snowman—right after breakfast the next morning.

Now I am going to ask you some questions about the story. For each question that I ask, there are three pictures in a row. Draw a circle around the picture that shows the best answer. Listen carefully.

1. **Look at the first row of pictures at the top of the page where there is a square. Put your finger on the square. What was the weather like in this story?** *Sunny . . . snowy . . . or rainy?* **Draw a circle around the picture that shows what the weather was like.**

2. **Move down to the next row of pictures where you see the circle. Put your finger on the circle. What did Michael put on his feet before he went to Peter's house?** *Sandals . . . sneakers . . . or boots?* **Draw a circle around the picture that shows what Michael put on his feet.**

3. Move down to the next row where you see the triangle. Put your finger on the triangle. **Where did Michael put his backpack?** *On a sled . . . in the car . . . or in the closet?* Draw a circle around the picture that shows where Michael put his backpack.

4. Move down to the next row where you see the heart. Put your finger on the heart. **How did Michael get to Peter's house?** *By car . . . by walking . . . or by skating?* Draw a circle around the picture that shows how Michael got to Peter's house.

5. Move down to the last row where you see the rectangle. Put your finger on the rectangle. **When did this story happen?** *In the morning . . . at lunchtime . . . or at night?* Draw a circle around the picture that shows when the story happened.

Scoring: For each child, mark the answer to each question correct or incorrect. Then count the total number correct for each child. Using the guidelines below, record the child's score on the Individual Record for the Unit 2 Benchmark Assessment (T27).

Number Correct	Rating	
5	Proficient	+
3 – 4	Developing	✓
Less than 3	Emerging	–

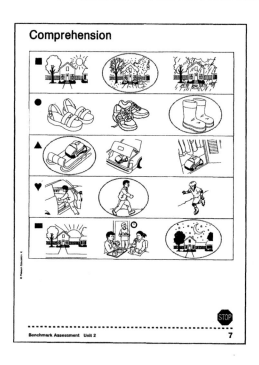

5. Writing: Nouns

(Individual, small group, or whole class)

Purpose: Assesses ability to draw a person, animal, place, or thing and write the noun that names it.

Hand out student page 8. Children will draw a picture and name it. If the child is unable to write the noun that names the picture, have him or her dictate the word to you and record it under the picture.

Now we are going to do something different. You are going to draw something for me. Remember that a noun is the name of a person, animal, place, or thing. Draw a picture of a noun you like. Then write its name under the picture.

Scoring: Using the guidelines below, evaluate the child's work and record the child's score on the Individual Record for the Unit 2 Benchmark Assessment (T27).

Scoring Guidelines	Rating	
The child draws a recognizable person, animal, place, or thing and writes the appropriate noun to identify the picture.	Proficient	+
The child draws a reasonable picture and writes some letters to the noun or can name it.	Developing	✓
The child draws a picture and attempts to write or name the noun, but both are less than complete and correct.	Emerging	−

Writing

8   Benchmark Assessment Unit 2

INDIVIDUAL RECORD

Unit 2 Benchmark Assessment

Child's Name _____ Date _____

Directions: Record the results of the Unit 2 Benchmark Assessment by marking Proficient (+), Developing (✓), or Emerging (−) beside each assessed skill.

Unit 2 Assessed Skills	Proficient (+)	Developing (✓)	Emerging (−)
Phonemic Awareness: Initial Sounds (/m/, /t/, short a, /s/, /p/, /k/ spelled c, short i)			
Phonics: Letter-Sound Correspondence (m, t, short a, s, p, c, short i)			
Word Knowledge: High-Frequency Words			
Listening Comprehension: Setting			
Writing: Nouns			

Notes/Observations

UNIT 3 DIRECTIONS

1. Phonemic Awareness: Initial Sounds (/b/, /n/, /r/, /d/, /k/, /f/, short o)

(Individual or small group)

Purpose: Assesses ability to recognize initial sounds.

Directions in **bold** are to be read aloud; others are for your information only.

Hand out student pages 2 and 3. Use the following directions to administer the test, beginning with the sample question.

Now we are going to listen to the beginning sound of a word. Let's do the first one together. Find the small star at the top of the page. Put your finger on it. Now look at the picture by the star. It is a *fish.* **The beginning sound in** *fish* **is /f/. Now look at the three pictures in the same row:** *bird, house, foot.* **Which word begins with the same sound as** *fish—bird, house, or foot?* (Pause.) **Yes,** *foot* **starts with the same sound as** *fish.* **Draw a circle around the picture of the foot because** *foot* **is the word that begins with the same sound as** *fish.*

When you are sure that each child understands the task and has followed the directions for completing the sample item, administer each test item.

1. **Move down to the next row where you see the picture of a** *book* **by the square. Put your finger on the square. Look at the pictures in the same row:** *bag, gate, pen.* **Circle the word that begins with the same sound as** *book . . . book.*

2. **Move down to the next row where you see the picture of the** *nest* **by the circle. Put your finger on the circle. Look at the pictures in the same row:** *mouse, top, nose.* **Circle the word that begins with the same sound as** *nest . . . nest.*

3. **Move down to the next row where you see the picture of the** *rake* **by the triangle. Put your finger on the triangle. Look at the pictures in the same row:** *cat, rose, bean.* **Circle the word that begins with the same sound as** *rake . . . rake.*

4. **Move down to the next row where you see the picture of the** *deer* **by the heart. Put your finger on the heart. Look at the pictures in the same row:** *pig, desk, box.* **Circle the word that begins with the same sound as** *deer . . . deer.*

5. **Now look at the next page. Go to the first row where you see the picture of the** *kite* **by the square. Put your finger on the square. Look at the pictures in the same row:** *key, bell, goat.* **Circle the word that begins with the same sound as** *kite . . . kite.*

6. **Move down to the next row where you see the picture of the _fork_ by the circle. Put your finger on the circle. Look at the pictures in the same row: _fence, leaf, pail._ Circle the word that begins with the same sound as _fork_ . . . _fork._**

7. **Move down to the last row where you see the picture of the _ox_ by the triangle. Put your finger on the triangle. Look at the pictures in the same row: _ape, octopus, eagle._ Circle the word that begins with the same sound as _ox_ . . . _ox._**

Scoring: For each child, mark the answer to each question correct or incorrect. Then count the total number correct for each child. Using the guidelines below, record the child's score on the Individual Record for the Unit 3 Benchmark Assessment (T37).

Number Correct	Rating	
7	Proficient	+
5 – 6	Developing	✓
Less than 5	Emerging	–

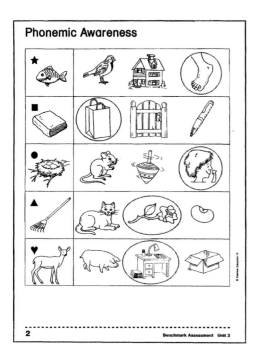

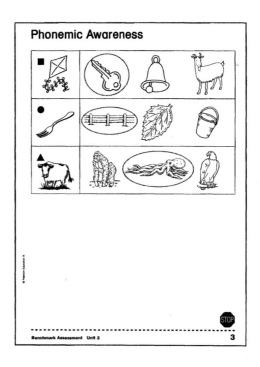

2. Phonics: Letter-Sound Correspondence (b, n, r, d, k, f, short o)

(Individual or small group)

Purpose: Assesses ability to connect sound to letter.

Hand out student pages 4 and 5. Use the following directions to administer the assessment, beginning with the sample question.

Now we are going to find the letter for a sound. Let's do the first one together. Find the small star at the top of the page. Put your finger on it. Now look at the picture by the star. It is a picture of a *mat*. The first sound in *mat* is /m/. Now look at the letters in the same row. What is the letter for /m/? (Pause) **Yes, the first letter in the row is the letter for /m/. Draw a circle around the *m*.**

When you are sure that each child understands the task and has followed the directions for completing the sample item, administer each test item.

1. **Move down to the next row where you see the square. Put your finger on the square. Look at the picture of the *bed*. The first sound in *bed* is /b/. What is the letter for /b/? Circle the letter for /b/.**

2. **Move down to the next row where you see the circle. Put your finger on the circle. Look at the picture of the *nail*. The first sound in *nail* is /n/. What is the letter for /n/? Circle the letter for /n/.**

3. **Move down to the next row where you see the triangle. Put your finger on the triangle. Look at the picture of the *rabbit*. The first sound in *rabbit* is /r/. What is the letter for /r/? Circle the letter for /r/.**

4. **Move down to the next row where you see the heart. Put your finger on the heart. Look at the picture of the *dog*. The first sound in *dog* is /d/. What is the letter for /d/? Circle the letter for /d/.**

5. **Now look at the next page. Go to the first row where you see the square. Put your finger on the square. Look at the picture of the *kite*. The first sound in *kite* is /k/. What is the letter for /k/? Circle the letter for /k/.**

6. **Move down to the next row where you see the circle. Put your finger on the circle. Look at the picture of the *fan*. The first sound in *fan* is /f/. What is the letter for /f/? Circle the letter for /f/.**

7. **Move down to the last row where you see the triangle. Put your finger on the triangle. Look at the picture of the *pot*. The middle sound in *pot* is /o/. What is the letter for /o/? Circle the letter for /o/.**

Scoring: For each child, mark the answer to each question correct or incorrect. Then count the total number correct for each child. Using the guidelines below, record the child's score on the Individual Record for the Unit 3 Benchmark Assessment (T37).

Number Correct	Rating	
7	Proficient	+
5 – 6	Developing	✓
Less than 5	Emerging	–

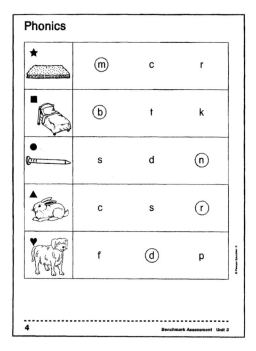

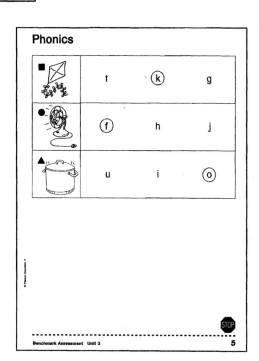

3. Word Knowledge: High-Frequency Words

(Individual or small group)

Purpose: Assesses ability to recognize high-frequency words.

Hand out student page 6. As you say a word aloud, the child will circle it. Move through the assessment quickly to make sure you are assessing the child's ability to recognize the high-frequency words quickly.

1. Now I am going to say one word in each row, and you are going to circle the word that I am saying. Find the star and put your finger on it. Now look at the three words in that row. Draw a circle around the word *me . . . me.*

2. Move down to the next row. Find the square. Put your finger on it. Look at the three words. Draw a circle around the word *with . . . with.*

3. Move down to the next row. Find the circle. Put your finger on it. Look at the three words. Circle the word *she . . . she.*

4. Move down to the next row. Find the triangle. Put your finger on it. Look at the three words. Circle the word *look . . . look.*

5. Move down to the next row. Find the heart. Put your finger on it. Look at the three words. Circle the word *see . . . see.*

6. Move down to the next row. Find the rectangle. Put your finger on it. Look at the three words. Circle the word *they . . . they.*

7. Move down to the next row. Find the diamond. Put your finger on it. Look at the three words. Circle the word *you . . . you.*

8. Move down to the next row. Find the oval. Put your finger on it. Look at the three words. Circle the word *of . . . of.*

Scoring: For each child, count the total number of words circled correctly. Using the guidelines below, record the child's score on the Individual Record for the Unit 3 Benchmark Assessment (T37).

Number Correct	Rating	
8	Proficient	+
5 – 7	Developing	✓
Less than 5	Emerging	–

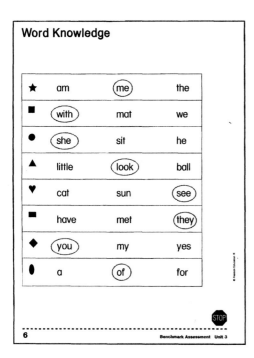

4. Listening Comprehension: Main Idea

(Individual, small group, or whole class)

Purpose: Assesses general comprehension.

Hand out student page 7. Read the story aloud. Then read each question that follows. Have children respond by circling the answer to each question.

Now I am going to read a story about a girl named Shari. Then I will ask you some questions. Listen carefully. Here is the story.

Shari was getting ready for the school play. First she put on black pants and a black shirt. Next she put a pair of pointy black ears on her head. Then she pinned a long black tail to her pants. Finally, she pasted a set of whiskers on her cheeks. When she was done, she looked in the mirror and smiled at herself. She was ready. She let out a loud meow and crept into the living room on her hands and knees.

Shari's family was waiting to see what she looked like. They all giggled as she meowed and meowed. But Jake the dog barked and barked. Shari thought that was strange. Jake never barked at her. Why was he barking now?

Next Jake did something even stranger. He ran up to Shari and started to tug on her tail. Shari's father rescued the tail from Jake's mouth.

"Stand up, Shari," said her father. "Jake thinks you're a cat. He wants to chase you."

Shari stood up. Sure enough, Jake stopped barking and tugging her tail.

"Well," said Shari's mother with a laugh, "that shows what a good cat you are. You're certainly ready for the school play."

Now I am going to ask you some questions about the story. For each question there are three pictures in a row. Draw a circle around the picture that shows the best answer. Listen carefully.

1. **Look at the first row of pictures at the top of the page where you see the square. Put your finger on the square. What kind of animal did Shari pretend to be? Draw a circle around the picture that shows what kind of animal Shari pretended to be.**

2. **Move down to the next row of pictures where you see the circle. Put your finger on the circle. What did Shari's family do when she meowed and meowed? Draw a circle that shows what Shari's family did when she meowed and meowed.**

3. **Move down to the next row of pictures where you see the triangle. Put your finger on the triangle. What did Jake the dog do when he saw Shari? Draw a circle around the picture that shows what Jake the dog did when he saw Shari.**

4. **Move down to the next row of pictures where you see the heart. Put your finger on the heart. How did Shari's dad help her? Draw a circle around the picture that shows what Shari's dad did to help her.**

5. Move down to the last row of pictures where you see the rectangle. Put your finger on the rectangle. Who told Shari to stand up? Draw a circle around the picture that shows who told Shari to stand up.

Scoring: For each child, mark the answer to each question correct or incorrect. Then count the total number correct for each child. Using the guidelines below, record the child's score on the Individual Record for the Unit 3 Benchmark Assessment (T37).

Number Correct	Rating	
5	Proficient	+
3 – 4	Developing	✓
Less than 3	Emerging	–

5. Writing: Verbs

(Individual, small group, or whole class)

Purpose: Assesses ability to write with a verb.

Hand out student page 8. Children will draw a picture and write an action verb under the picture. If you do not think that the child will be able to write the verb, have him or her dictate the word to you. Record the word on the page under the picture.

Remember that a verb is an action word. Draw a picture of yourself or an animal doing something. Then label the picture using a verb.

Scoring: Using the guidelines below, evaluate the child's work and record the child's score on the Individual Record for the Unit 3 Benchmark Assessment (T37).

Scoring Guidelines	Rating	
The child draws a recognizable picture and writes the appropriate verb to identify the picture.	Proficient	+
The child draws a reasonable picture and writes some letters of the verb or can dictate it.	Developing	✓
The child draws a picture and attempts to write or dictate the verb, but both are less than complete and correct.	Emerging	–

Writing

STOP

8   Benchmark Assessment Unit 3

INDIVIDUAL RECORD

Unit 3 Benchmark Assessment

Child's Name _____ **Date** _____

Directions: Record the results of the Unit 3 Benchmark Assessment by marking Proficient (+), Developing (✓), or Emerging (–) beside each assessed skill.

Unit 3 Assessed Skills	Proficient (+)	Developing (✓)	Emerging (–)
Phonemic Awareness: Initial sounds (/b/, /n/, /r/, /d/, /k/, /f/, short o)			
Phonics: Letter-Sound Correspondence (b, n, r, d, k, f, short o)			
Word Knowledge: High-Frequency Words			
Listening Comprehension: Main Idea			
Writing: Verbs			

Notes/Observations

UNIT 4 DIRECTIONS

1. Phonemic Awareness: Initial and Final Sounds
(Individual or small group)

Purpose: Assesses ability to recognize initial and final sounds, including some consonant blends.

Hand out student pages 2–3. Use the following directions to administer the test, beginning with the sample question. Directions in **bold** are to be read aloud. The others are for your information only.

Now you are going to listen to sounds in words. Let's do the first one together. Find the small star. Put your finger on it. Now look at the three pictures in the row beside the star: *heart, hand, giraffe.* **Listen to the beginning sound of each word:** *heart, hand, giraffe.* **Two of the words begin with the same sound. One of the words begins with a different sound. Which two words have the same beginning sound?** (Pause.) **Yes,** *heart* **and** *hand* **have the same beginning sound. Draw a circle around the pictures of the** *heart* **and the** *hand.*

When you are sure that each child understands the task and has followed the directions for completing the sample item, administer each test item.

1. **Move down to the next row where you see the square. Put your finger on the square. Now look at the pictures in the same row:** *tree, car, truck.* **Circle the pictures that have the same sound at the beginning:** *tree . . . car . . . truck.*

2. **Move down to the next row where you see the circle. Put your finger on the circle. Look at the pictures:** *elephant, egg, ox.* **Circle the pictures that have the same sound at the beginning:** *elephant . . . egg . . . ox.*

3. **Move down to the next row where you see the triangle. Put your finger on the triangle. Look at the pictures:** *spoon, bread, spider.* **Circle the pictures that have the same sound at the beginning:** *spoon . . . bread . . . spider.*

4. **Move down to the next row where you see the heart. Put your finger on the heart. Look at the pictures:** *broom, drum, dress.* **Circle the pictures that have the same sound at the beginning:** *broom . . . drum . . . dress.*

5. **Go to the top of the next page. Look at the top row where you see the square. Put your finger on the square. Look at the pictures:** *hat, goat, house.* **Circle the pictures that have the same sound at the beginning:** *hat . . . goat . . . house.*

6. **Move down to the next row where you see the circle. Put your finger on the circle. Look at the pictures. Listen for the last sound:** *rake, ball, nail.* **Circle the pictures that have the same sound at the end:** *rake . . . ball . . . nail.*

7. **Move down to the next row where you see the triangle. Put your finger on the triangle. Look at the pictures. Listen for the last sound:** *bag, pig, cup.* **Circle the pictures that have the same sound at the end:** *bag . . . pig . . . cup.*

8. **Move down to the last row where you see the heart. Put your finger on the heart. Look at the pictures. Listen for the last sound:** *nest, milk, fist.* **Circle the pictures that have the same sound at the end:** *nest . . . milk . . . fist.*

Scoring: For each child, mark the answer to each question correct or incorrect. Then count the total number correct for each child. Using the guidelines below, record the child's score on the Individual Record for the Unit 4 Benchmark Assessment (T49).

Number Correct	Rating	
8	Proficient	+
6 – 7	Developing	✓
Less than 6	Emerging	–

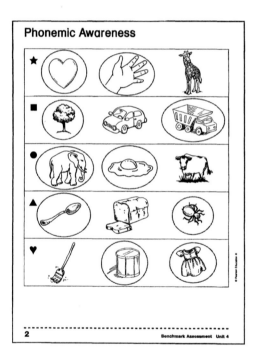

© Pearson Education **K**

2. Phonics: Letter-Sound Correspondence (h, l, g, short e, st-, sp-, tr-, bl-, br-, dr-, -st, -sp, -lk)

(Individual or small group)

Purpose: Assesses ability to connect sound to letter.

Hand out student pages 4–5. Use the following directions to administer the assessment, beginning with the sample question.

Now we are going to find letters for a sound. Let's do the first one together. Find the small star. Put your finger on it. Now look at the picture by the star. It is a picture of a *tree*. The beginning sound in *tree* is /tr/. Now look at the letters in the same row. Which are the letters for the sound /tr/? (Pause.) Yes, the last two letters in the row are the letters for the sound /tr/. Draw a circle around the letters *tr* because those are the letters for the sound /tr/.

When you are sure that each child understands the task and has followed the directions for completing the sample item, administer each test item.

1. **Move down to the next row where you see a square. Put your finger on the square. Look at the picture of the *spoon* by the square. The beginning sound in *spoon* is /sp/. What are the letters for the sound /sp/? Circle the letters for the sound /sp/.**

2. **Move down to the next row where you see a circle. Put your finger on the circle. Look at the picture of the *broom* by the circle. The beginning sound in *broom* is /br/. What are the letters for the sound /br/? Circle the letters for the sound /br/.**

3. **Move down to the next row where you see a triangle. Put your finger on the triangle. Look at the picture of the *leaf* by the triangle. The beginning sound in *leaf* is /l/. What is the letter for the sound /l/? Circle the letter for the sound /l/.**

4. **Move down to the next row where you see a heart. Put your finger on the heart. Look at the picture of the *egg* by the heart. The beginning sound in *egg* is /e/. What is the letter for the sound /e/? Circle the letter for the sound /e/.**

5. **Turn to the next page. Look at the top row where you see a square. Put your finger on the square. Look at the picture of the *house* by the square. The beginning sound in *house* is /h/. What is the letter for the sound /h/? Circle the letter for the sound /h/.**

6. **Move down to the next row where you see a circle. Put your finger on the circle. Look at the picture of the *dog* by the circle. The final sound in *dog* is /g/. What is the letter for the sound /g/? Circle the letter for the sound /g/.**

© Pearson Education K

7. **Move down to the next row where you see a triangle. Put your finger on the triangle. Look at the picture of *milk* by the triangle. The final sound in *milk* is /lk/. What are the letters for the sound /lk/? Circle the letters for the sound /lk/.**

8. **Move down to the last row where you see a heart. Put your finger on the heart. Look at the picture of *toast* by the heart. The final sound in *toast* is /st/. What are the letters for the sound /st/? Circle the letters for the sound /st/.**

Scoring: For each child, mark the answer to each question correct or incorrect. Then count the total number correct for each child. Using the guidelines below, record the child's score on the Individual Record for the Unit 4 Benchmark Assessment (T49).

Number Correct	Rating	
8	Proficient	+
6 – 7	Developing	✓
Less than 6	Emerging	–

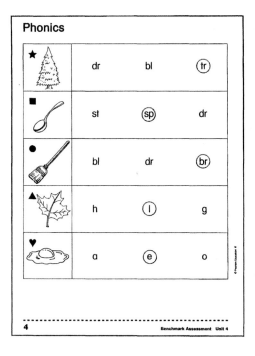

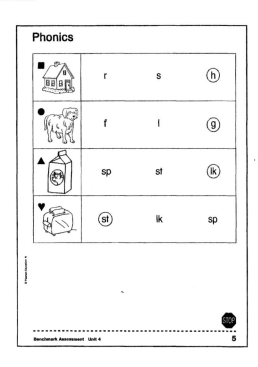

3. Word Reading

(Individual or small group)

Purpose: Assesses ability to read CVC words.

Hand out student page 6. Use the following directions to administer the assessment, beginning with the sample question.

Now we are going to find some words you know. Let's do the first one together. Find the small star. Put your finger on it. Now look at the picture by the star. It is a *cat*. Look at the three words in the same row. Which word spells *cat*? (Pause.) **Yes, the first word in the row is *cat*. Cat is spelled *c, a, t*. Draw a circle around the word *cat*.**

When you are sure that each child understands the task and has followed the directions for completing the sample item, administer each test item.

1. **Move down to the next row where you see the square. Put your finger on the square. Look at the picture. It is a *bed*. Look at the words in the row. Circle the word *bed*.**

2. **Move down to the next row where you see the circle. Put your finger on the circle. Look at the picture. It is a *hat*. Look at the words in the row. Circle the word *hat*.**

3. **Move down to the next row where you see the triangle. Put your finger on the triangle. Look at the picture. It is a *net*. Look at the words in the row. Circle the word *net*.**

4. **Move down to the next row where you see the heart. Put your finger on the heart. Look at the picture. It is a *top*. Look at the words in the row. Circle the word *top*.**

5. **Move down to the last row where you see the rectangle. Put your finger on the rectangle. Look at the picture. It is a *pin*. Look at the words in the row. Circle the word *pin*.**

Scoring: For each child, mark the answer to each question correct or incorrect. Then count the total number correct for each child. Using the guidelines below, record the child's score on the Individual Record for the Unit 4 Benchmark Assessment (T49).

Number Correct	Rating	
5	Proficient	+
3 – 4	Developing	✓
Less than 3	Emerging	–

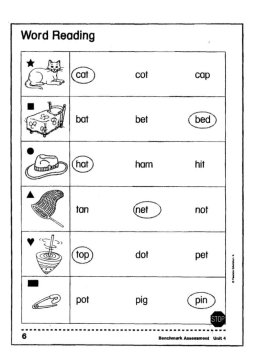

Word Reading

★	(cat)	cot	cap
■	bat	bet	(bed)
●	(hat)	ham	hit
▲	tan	(net)	not
♥	(top)	dot	pet
■	pot	pig	(pin)

6 Benchmark Assessment Unit 4

4. Word Knowledge: High-Frequency Words

(Individual or small group)

Purpose: Assesses ability to recognize high-frequency words.

Hand out student pages 7–8.

1. Let's find some words you know. I am going to say a word and ask you to draw a circle around that word. Find the star in the top row. Put your finger on it. Now look at the three words in that row. Draw a circle around the word *are . . . are.*

2. Move down to the next row with a square. Put your finger on the square. Look at the three words. Draw a circle around the word *that . . . that.*

3. Move down to the next row with a circle. Put your finger on the circle. Look at the three words. Circle the word *do . . . do.*

4. Move down to the next row with a triangle. Put your finger on the triangle. Look at the three words. Circle the word *one . . . one.*

5. Move down to the next row with a heart. Put your finger on the heart. Look at the three words. Circle the word *two . . . two.*

6. Move down to the next row with a rectangle. Put your finger on the rectangle. Look at the three words. Circle the word *three . . . three.*

7. Move down to the next row with a diamond. Put your finger on the diamond. Look at the three words. Circle the word *four . . . four.*

8. Move down to the next row with an oval. Put your finger on the oval. Look at the three words. Circle the word *five . . . five.*

9. Now go to the top of the next page. Look at the top row with a square. Put your finger on the square. Look at the three words. Circle the word *here . . . here.*

10. Move down to the next row with a circle. Put your finger on the circle. Look at the three words. Circle the word *go . . . go.*

11. Move down to the last row, with a triangle. Put your finger on the triangle. Look at the three words. Circle the word *from . . . from.*

Scoring: For each child, count the total number of words circled correctly. Using the guidelines below, record the child's score on the Individual Record for the Unit 4 Benchmark Assessment (T49).

Number Correct	Rating	
11	Proficient	+
8 – 10	Developing	✓
Less than 8	Emerging	–

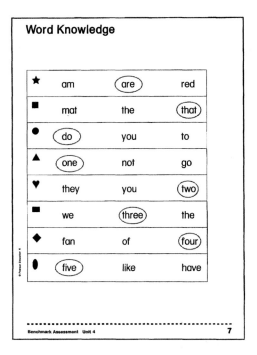

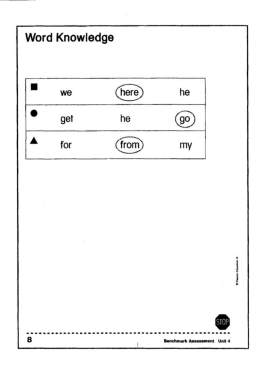

5. Listening Comprehension: Sequence

(Individual, small group or whole class)

Hand out student page 9. Read aloud the introduction and the story printed in **bold.** Then read each question that follows. Children are to respond by circling the best answer to each question.

I am going to read a story about Ricky's mother and her hobby. Then I will ask you some questions. Listen carefully. Here is the story.

Ricky's mother had a very special hobby. She was a clown, but she didn't work in a circus. Instead, she went to children's hospitals to help the sick children feel better. She did that by making them laugh.

Every Saturday, Ricky's mother put on great big clothes and great big clown shoes. She painted a great big smile on her face. Then she gathered her bag of tricks. She had balloons. She had balls. She had a puppet that looked like a white rabbit. Ricky helped out by putting the bag in her car.

Then Ricky's mother drove to the hospital. People laughed and waved when they saw her in her car.

At the hospital, Ricky's mother put on a show. First she twisted the balloons into funny animals. She gave one to every child. Then she juggled the balls. She hardly ever dropped one. Finally, she made the puppet wiggle its rabbit nose and rabbit ears. She made the puppet talk too. He told jokes in a funny voice.

The children laughed and laughed. They clapped and clapped. By the time the show was over, they really did feel better. Ricky's mother felt good too.

Now I am going to ask you some questions about the story. For each question there are three pictures. Draw a circle around the picture that shows the best answer. Listen carefully.

1. Look at the first row of pictures at the top of the page where you see the square. Put your finger on the square. What does Ricky's mother do first in the story? Draw a circle around the picture that shows what Ricky's mother does first.

2. Move down to the next row of pictures where you see the circle. Put your finger on the circle. What kind of clown face does Ricky's mother paint on—sad, happy, or angry? Draw a circle around the picture that shows what kind of clown face she paints on.

3. Move down to the next row of pictures where you see the triangle. Put your finger on the triangle. What did people do when they saw Ricky's mother in her car? Draw a circle around the picture that shows what people did when they saw Ricky's mother in her car.

© Pearson Education K

4. Move down to the next row of pictures where you see the heart. Put your finger on the heart. What did Ricky do to help his mother? Draw a circle around the picture that shows how Ricky helped his mother.

5. Move down to the last row of pictures where you see the rectangle. Put your finger on the rectangle. What happened last in the story? Draw a circle around the picture that shows what happened last in the story.

Scoring: For each child, mark the answer to each question correct or incorrect. Then count the total number correct for each child. Using the guidelines below, record the child's score on the Individual Record for the Unit 4 Benchmark Assessment (T49).

Number Correct	Rating	
5	Proficient	+
3 – 4	Developing	✓
Less than 3	Emerging	–

© Pearson Education K

6. Writing: Sentences

(Individual, small group, or whole class)

Purpose: Assesses ability to write a sentence

Hand out student page 10. Instruct children as follows.

Think about an adventure we have read about. Draw a picture about the adventure. Then write a sentence that tells about the picture.

Note: If children have trouble thinking of an adventure, remind them of some of the stories that they have read in the classroom.

Scoring: Using the guidelines below, evaluate the child's work and record the child's score on the Individual Record for the Unit 4 Benchmark Assessment (T49).

Scoring Guidelines	Rating	
The child draws a recognizable picture and writes a sentence that tells about the picture.	Proficient	+
The child draws a reasonable picture and writes some words or can dictate a sentence.	Developing	✓
The child draws a picture and attempts to write or dictate a sentence, but both are less than complete and correct.	Emerging	–

Writing

STOP

10   Benchmark Assessment Unit 4

INDIVIDUAL RECORD

Unit 4 Benchmark Assessment

Child's Name _____ Date _____

Directions: Record the results of the Unit 4 Benchmark Assessment by marking
Proficient (+), Developing (✓), or Emerging (–) beside each assessed skill.

Unit 4 Assessed Skills	Proficient (+)	Developing (✓)	Emerging (–)
Phonemic Awareness: Recognizing Initial and Final Sounds			
Phonics: Letter-Sound Correspondence (h, l, g, short e, st-, sp-, tr-, bl-, br-, dr-, -st, -sp, -lk)			
Word Reading: CVC Words			
Word Knowledge: High-Frequency Words			
Listening Comprehension: Sequence			
Writing: Sentences			

Notes/Observations

UNIT 5 DIRECTIONS

1. Phonemic Awareness: Recognizing Initial and Final Sounds (/w/, /j/, short u, /v/, /z/, /y/, /kw/) and Final Sounds (-/x/, -/z/)

(Individual or small group)

Purpose: Assesses ability to recognize initial sounds and final sounds.

Hand out student pages 2–3. Use the following directions to administer the test, beginning with the sample question. Directions in **bold** are to be read aloud. The others are for your information only.

We are going to listen for sounds in words. Find the small star. Put your finger on it. Now look at the three pictures in the row beside the star: *jacks, whale, jam.* **Listen to the beginning sound of each word:** *jacks, whale, jam.* **Two of the words begin with the same sound. One of the words begins with a different sound. Which two words have the same beginning sound?** (Pause.) **Yes,** *jacks* **and** *jam* **have the same beginning sound. Draw a circle around the pictures of the** *jacks* **and the** *jam.*

When you are sure that each child understands the task and has followed the directions for completing the sample item, administer each test item.

1. **Move down to the next row where you see the square. Put your finger on the square. Now look at the three pictures in the same row:** *web, wing, horse.* **Draw a circle around the two pictures that have the same sound at the beginning:** *web . . . wing . . . horse.*

2. **Move down to the next row where you see the circle. Put your finger on the circle. Look at the three pictures in that row:** *violin, nail, van.* **Draw a circle around the two pictures that have the same sound at the beginning:** *violin . . . nail . . . van.*

3. **Move down to the next row where you see the triangle. Put your finger on the triangle. Look at the three pictures in that row:** *jar, jet, goat.* **Draw a circle around the two pictures that have the same sound at the beginning:** *jar . . . jet . . . goat.*

4. **Move down to the next row where you see the heart. Put your finger on the heart. Look at the three pictures in that row:** *apple, umbrella, up.* **Draw a circle around the two pictures that have the same sound at the beginning:** *apple . . . umbrella . . . up.*

5. **Go to the top of the next page. Look at the top row where you see the square. Put your finger on the square. Look at the three pictures in that row:** *zebra, monkey, zipper.* **Draw a circle around the two pictures that have the same sound at the beginning:** *zebra . . . monkey . . . zipper.*

© Pearson Education K

6. Move down to the next row where you see the circle. Put your finger on the circle. Look at the three pictures in that row: *watch, yo-yo, yarn*. Draw a circle around the two pictures that have the same sound at the beginning: *watch . . . yo-yo . . . yarn.*

7. Move down to the next row where you see the triangle. Put your finger on the triangle. Look at the three pictures in that row: *fence, queen, quilt*. Draw a circle around the two pictures that have the same sound at the beginning: *fence . . . queen . . . quilt.*

8. Move down to the next row where you see the heart. Put your finger on the heart. Look at the three pictures in that row. Listen for the ending sound: *rose, sock, sneeze*. Draw a circle around the two pictures that have the same sound at the end: *rose . . . sock . . . sneeze.*

9. Move down to the last row where you see the rectangle. Put your finger on the rectangle. Look at the three pictures in that row. Listen for the ending sound: *box, kite, six*. Draw a circle around the two pictures that have the same sound at the end: *box . . . kite . . . six.*

Scoring: For each child, mark the answer to each question correct or incorrect. Then count the total number correct for each child. Using the guidelines below, record the child's score on the Individual Record for the Unit 5 Benchmark Assessment (T62).

Number Correct	Rating	
9	Proficient	+
7 – 8	Developing	✓
Less than 7	Emerging	–

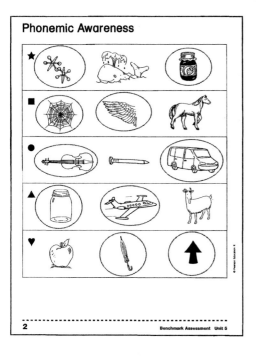

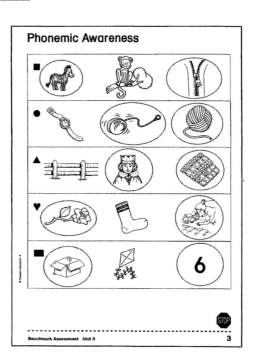

© Pearson Education **K**

2. Phonics: Letter-Sound Correspondence (w, j, v, y, qu, short u, -x, -z)

(Individual or small group)

Purpose: Assesses ability to connect sound to letter.

Hand out student pages 4–5. Use the following directions to administer the assessment, beginning with the sample question.

Now we are going to match a letter to its sound. Let's do the first one together. Find the small star. Put your finger on it. Now look at the letter by the star. It is a the letter *j*. What is the sound of the letter *j*? (Have a child give the sound of the letter *j*.) **Now look at the three pictures in the same row: *sun, jar, fish*. Which word begins with the sound of the letter *j*?** (Pause.) **Yes, *jar* begins with the sound of the letter *j*. Draw a circle around the picture of the *jar* because *jar* begins with the letter *j*.**

When you are sure that each child understands the task and has followed the directions for completing the sample item, administer each test item.

1. **Move down to the next row where you see the square. Put your finger on the square. Look at the *w*. Look at the pictures: *worm, bird, vest*. Circle the picture that begins with the sound of the letter *w*.**

2. **Move down to the next row where you see the circle. Put your finger on the circle. Look at the *u*. Look at the pictures: *egg, umbrella, igloo*. Circle the picture that begins with the sound of the letter *u*.**

3. **Move down to the next row where you see the triangle. Put your finger on the triangle. Look at the *v*. Look at the pictures: *van, whale, ten*. Circle the picture that begins with the sound of the letter *v*.**

4. **Move down to the next row where you see the heart. Put your finger on the heart. Look at the *y*. Look at the pictures: *yarn, pen, fence*. Circle the picture that begins with the sound of the letter *y*.**

5. **Go to the next page. Look at the top row where you see the square. Put your finger on the square. Look at the *qu*. Look at the pictures: *hen, queen, vase*. Circle the picture that begins with the sound of the letters *qu*.**

6. **Move down to the next row where you see the circle. Put your finger on the circle. Look at the *j*. Look at the pictures: *bus, train, jet*. Circle the picture that begins with the sound of the letter *j*.**

7. **Move down to the next row where you see the triangle. Put your finger on the triangle. Look at the *x*. Look at the pictures. Listen for the ending sound: *fox, mat, dog*. Circle the picture that ends with the sound of the letter *x*.**

© Pearson Education K

8. Move down to the next row where you see the heart. Put your finger on the heart. Look at the pictures. Listen for the ending sound: *goat, hand, maze.* Circle the picture that ends with the sound of the letter *z.*

Scoring: For each child, mark the answer to each question correct or incorrect. Then count the total number correct for each child. Using the guidelines below, record the child's score on the Individual Record for the Unit 5 Benchmark Assessment (T62).

Number Correct	Rating	
8	Proficient	+
6 – 7	Developing	✓
Less than 6	Emerging	–

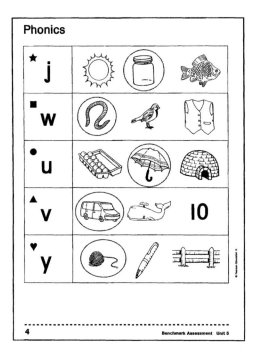

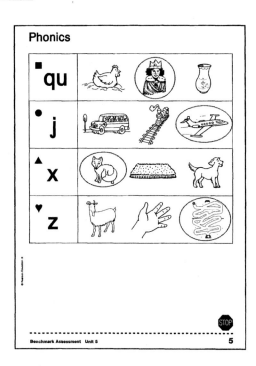

3. Word Reading

(Individual or small group)

Purpose: Assesses ability to read CVC words.

Hand out student pages 6–7. Use the following directions to administer the assessment, beginning with the sample question.

Now we are going to circle some words you know. Let's do the first one together. Find the small star. Put your finger on it. Now look at the picture by the star. It is a *cup*. Now look at the three words in the same row. Which word spells *cup*? (Pause.) **Yes, the last word in the row is *cup*. *Cup* is spelled *c, u, p . . . cup*. Draw a circle around the word *cup*.**

When you are sure that each child understands the task and has followed the directions for completing the sample item, administer each test item.

1. **Move down to the next row where you see the square. Put your finger on it. Look at the picture. It is a *pin*. Look at the words in the row. Circle the word *pin*.**

2. **Move down to the next row where you see the circle. Put your finger on it. Look at the picture. It is a *bat*. Look at the words in the row. Circle the word *bat*.**

3. **Move down to the next row where you see the triangle. Put your finger on it. Look at the picture. It is the number *ten*. Look at the words in the row. Circle the word *ten*.**

4. **Move down to the next row where you see the heart. Put your finger on it. Look at the picture. It is a *box*. Look at the words in the row. Circle the word *box*.**

5. **Go to the next page. Look at the top row where you see the square. Put your finger on it. Look at the picture. It is a *log*. Look at the words in the row. Circle the word *log*.**

6. **Move down to the next row where you see the circle. Put your finger on it. Look at the picture. It is a *man*. Look at the words in the row. Circle the word *man*.**

7. **Move down to the next row where you see the triangle. Put your finger on it. Look at the picture. It is a *sun*. Look at the words in the row. Circle the word *sun*.**

8. **Move down to the last row where you see the heart. Put your finger on it. Look at the picture. It is a *bib*. Look at the words in the row. Circle the word *bib*.**

Scoring: For each child, mark the answer to each question correct or incorrect. Then count the total number correct for each child. Using the guidelines below, record the child's score on the Individual Record for the Unit 5 Benchmark Assessment (T62).

Number Correct	Rating	
8	Proficient	+
6 – 7	Developing	✓
Less than 6	Emerging	–

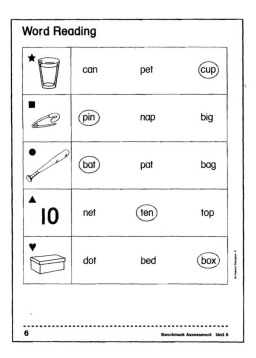

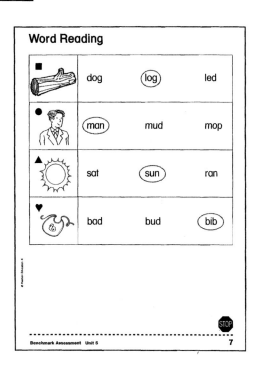

4. Word Knowledge: High-Frequency Words
(Individual or small group)

Purpose: Assesses ability to recognize high-frequency words.

Hand out page 8. Children are to circle each word as you say it aloud.

Now we are going to circle some words you know. Find the square. Put your finger on it. Now look at the three words in that row. Draw a circle around the word *yellow . . . yellow.*

Move down to the next row. Find the circle. Put your finger on it. Look at the three words. Circle the word *green . . . green.*

Move down to the next row. Find the triangle. Put your finger on it. Look at the three words. Circle the word *blue . . . blue.*

Move down to the next row. Find the heart. Put your finger on it. Look at the three words. Circle the word *what . . . what.*

Move down to the next row. Find the rectangle. Put your finger on it. Look at the three words. Circle the word *said . . . said.*

Move down to the next row. Find the diamond. Put your finger on it. Look at the three words. Circle the word *was . . . was.*

Move down to the next row. Find the oval. Put your finger on it. Look at the three words. Circle the word *where . . . where.*

Move down to the last row. Find the stop-sign shape. Put your finger on it. Look at the three words. Circle the word *come . . . come.*

Scoring: For each child, count the total number of words circled correctly. Using the guidelines below, record the child's score on the Individual Record for the Unit 5 Benchmark Assessment (T62).

Number Correct	Rating	
8	Proficient	+
6 – 7	Developing	✓
Less than 6	Emerging	–

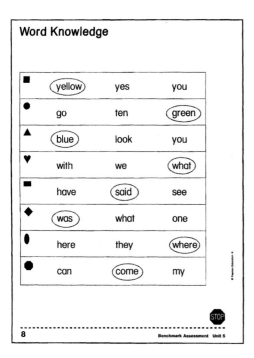

Word Knowledge

■	(yellow)	yes	you
●	go	ten	(green)
▲	(blue)	look	you
♥	with	we	(what)
■	have	(said)	see
◆	(was)	what	one
◖	here	they	(where)
●	can	(come)	my

STOP

8   Benchmark Assessment   Unit 5

5. Listening Comprehension: Plot

(Individual, small group, or whole class)

Hand out student page 9. Read aloud the introduction and the story printed in **bold.** Then read each question that follows. Children are to respond by circling the best answer to each question.

I am going to read a story about a king and his cook. Then I will ask you some questions. Listen carefully. Here is the story.

    Once upon a time there was a king named Frederick who lived in a tall castle high on a bright green hill. King Frederick had a fine white horse to ride, a bright golden crown to wear, a lot of money, and a cook to bring him tasty meals.

    But King Frederick was not happy.

    "I am so bored it makes me angry!" he told the castle cook one day. "I do not like being king anymore."

    The cook's name was Martin. "What would you like to be instead?" Martin the cook asked.

    King Frederick looked down at the tasty meal that Martin had set before him. The meat and vegetables smelled so delicious.

    "I know," said King Frederick to Martin the cook. "I would like to do what you do. Let's trade places, Martin. What do you say?"

    "Oh yes," Martin said, for he had always dreamed of being king.

    So Frederick gave Martin his crown and went skipping happily off to the kitchen. Now he, Frederick, was the castle cook. Meanwhile, Martin put on the heavy crown and sat on the golden throne. Now he, Martin, was king. "Hooray for King Martin!" Martin shouted.

    But King Martin soon grew lonesome, sitting on the throne under that heavy crown all day long. Martin missed his meats and vegetables and pots and pans. He wanted to be Martin the cook again. Meanwhile, Frederick was growing lonesome too. Cooking was hard work. He missed his fine white horse and golden crown. He wanted to be Frederick the king again.

    So the next day, the two men agreed to trade places again and go back to being their old selves. Frederick became King Frederick again, wearing his golden crown, and Martin became the castle cook again, making the king's meals like always, with a big, happy smile on his face.

Now I am going to ask you some questions about the story. For each question there are three pictures. Draw a circle around the picture that shows the best answer. Listen carefully.

1. Look at the first row of pictures where you see the square. Put your finger on the square. Who is this story about? Draw a circle around the picture that shows who this story is about.

2. Move down to the next row of pictures where you see the circle. Put your finger on the circle. How did King Frederick feel at the beginning of the story—happy, angry, or silly? Draw a circle around the picture that shows how King Frederick felt at the beginning of the story.

3. Move down to the next row of pictures where you see the triangle. Put your finger on the triangle. What did King Frederick give to Martin, his cook? Draw a circle around the picture that shows what King Frederick gave to his cook.

4. Move down to the next row of pictures where you see the heart. Put your finger on the heart. After trading places with King Frederick, what did Martin do all day long? Draw a circle around the picture that shows what Martin did all day long after trading places with the king.

5. Move down to the last row of pictures where you see the rectangle. Put your finger on the rectangle. How did Martin feel at the end of the story—happy, tired, or scared? Draw a circle around the picture that shows how Martin felt at the end of the story.

© Pearson Education K

Scoring: For each child, mark the answer to each question correct or incorrect. Then count the total number correct for each child. Using the guidelines below, record the child's score on the Individual Record for the Unit 5 Benchmark Assessment (T62).

Number Correct	Rating	
5	Proficient	+
3 – 4	Developing	✓
Less than 3	Emerging	–

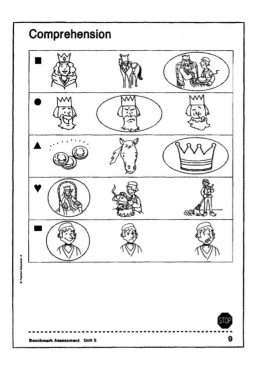

6. Writing: Questions

(Individual, small group, or whole class)

Purpose: Assesses ability to write a question

Hand out student page 10. Instruct children as follows.

Think about how you travel from place to place. Draw a picture of what you go on to get from one place to another. Then write a question about the picture.

Note: If children have trouble thinking of how they travel from place to place, talk briefly about forms of transportation.

Scoring: Using the guidelines below, evaluate the child's work and record the child's score on the Individual Record for the Unit 5 Benchmark Assessment (T62).

Scoring Guidelines	Rating	
The picture shows a form of transportation. The question is appropriate and generally written correctly.	Proficient	+
The picture is recognizable. There is a question or part of a question about the picture, but words may include a few errors.	Developing	✓
There is an attempt to draw a picture and write the question, but both are less than complete and correct.	Emerging	–

INDIVIDUAL RECORD

Unit 5 Benchmark Assessment

Child's Name _____ **Date** _____

Directions: Record the results of the Unit 5 Benchmark Assessment by marking Proficient (+), Developing (✓), or Emerging (–) beside each assessed skill.

Unit 5 Assessed Skills	Proficient (+)	Developing (✓)	Emerging (–)
Phonemic Awareness: Recognizing Initial Sounds and Final Sounds (/w/, /j/, short u, /v/, /z/, /y/, /kw/, -/x/, -/z/)			
Phonics: Letter-Sound Correspondence: (w, j, v, y, qu, short u, -x, -z)			
Word Reading: CVC Words			
Word Knowledge: High-Frequency Words			
Listening Comprehension: Plot			
Writing: Questions			

Notes/Observations

UNIT 6 DIRECTIONS

1. Phonemic Awareness: Blending Individual Phonemes
(Individual or small group)

Purpose: Assesses ability to blend individual phonemes.

Hand out student pages 2–3. Use the following directions to administer the test, beginning with the sample question.

We are going to listen to sounds in a word. Find the small star. Put your finger on it. Now look at the three pictures in that row. I am going to say a word. Listen to the sounds I say: /k/ /a/ /p/. Blend the sounds together. What word is it? (Pause.) **Yes, the word is** *cap.* **Which picture goes with the word /k/ /a/ /p/? Yes, the middle picture is a /k/ /a/ /p/ . . .** *cap.* **Draw a circle around the middle picture of the cap.**

When you are sure that each child understands the task and has followed the directions for completing the sample item, administer each test item.

1. **Move down to the next row where you see the square. Put your finger on it. Look at the three pictures in that row. Which picture is a /f/ /o/ /x/? Circle the picture of the /f/ /o/ /x/.**

2. **Move down to the next row where you see the circle. Put your finger on it. Look at the three pictures in that row. Which picture is a /h/ /i/ /l/? Circle the picture of the /h/ /i/ /l/.**

3. **Move down to the next row where you see the triangle. Put your finger on it. Look at the three pictures in that row. Which picture is a /b/ /a/ /g/? Circle the picture of the /b/ /a/ /g/.**

4. **Move down to the next row where you see the heart. Put your finger on it. Look at the three pictures in that row. Which picture is a /n/ /e/ /s/ /t/? Circle the picture of the /n/ /e/ /s/ /t/.**

5. **Go to the next page. Look at the top row where you see the square. Put your finger on it. Look at the three pictures in that row. Which picture is a /p/ /e/ /n/? Circle the picture of the /p/ /e/ /n/.**

6. **Move down to the next row where you see the circle. Put your finger on it. Look at the three pictures in that row. Which picture is a /w/ /e/ /b/? Circle the picture of the /w/ /e/ /b/.**

7. **Move down to the next row where you see the triangle. Put your finger on it. Look at the three pictures in that row. Which picture is a /t/ /r/ /u/ /k/? Circle the picture of the /t/ /r/ /u/ /k/.**

8. Move down to the last row where you see the heart. Put your finger on it. Look at the three pictures in that row. Which picture is a /v/ /e/ /s/ /t/? Circle the picture of the /v/ /e/ /s/ /t/.

Scoring: For each child, mark the answer to each question correct or incorrect. Then count the total number correct for each child. Using the guidelines below, record the child's score on the Individual Record for the Unit 6 Benchmark Assessment (T72).

Number Correct	Rating	
8	Proficient	+
6 – 7	Developing	✓
Less than 6	Emerging	–

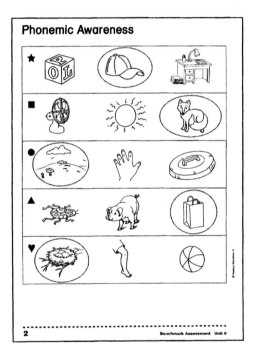

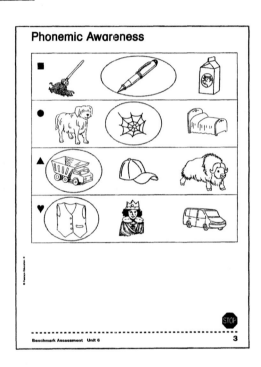

2. Word Reading

(Individual or small group)

Purpose: Assesses ability to read CVC, CVCC, and CCVC words.

Hand out student pages 4–5. Use the following directions to administer the assessment, beginning with the sample question.

Now we are going to circle words. Let's do the first one together. Find the small star. Put your finger on it. Now look at the picture by the star. It is a *pen*. Look at the three words in the same row. Which word is *pen*? (Pause.) **Yes, the middle word in the row is *pen: p, e, n . . . pen*. Draw a circle around the word *pen*.**

When you are sure that each child understands the task and has followed the directions for completing the sample item, administer each test item.

1. **Move down to the next row where you see the square. Put your finger on it. Look at the picture. It is a *step*. Look at the three words in the row. Circle the word *step . . . step*.**

2. **Move down to the next row where you see the circle. Put your finger on it. Look at the picture. It is a *bug*. Look at the three words in the row. Circle the word *bug . . . bug*.**

3. **Move down to the next row where you see the triangle. Put your finger on it. Look at the picture. It is a *fin*. Look at the three words in the row. Circle the word *fin . . . fin*.**

4. **Move down to the next row where you see the heart. Put your finger on it. Look at the picture. It is a *box*. Look at the three words in the row. Circle the word *box . . . box*.**

5. **Go to the next page. Look at the top row where you see the square. Put your finger on it. Look at the picture. It is a *jet*. Look at the three words in the row. Circle the word *jet . . . jet*.**

6. **Move down to the next row where you see the circle. Put your finger on it. Look at the picture. It is a *map*. Look at the three words in the row. Circle the word *map . . . map*.**

7. **Move down to the next row where you see the triangle. Put your finger on it. Look at the picture. It is a *tub*. Look at the three words in the row. Circle the word *tub . . . tub*.**

8. **Move down to the last row where you see the heart. Put your finger on it. Look at the picture. It is a *van*. Look at the three words in the row. Circle the word *van . . . van*.**

Scoring: For each child, mark the answer to each question correct or incorrect. Then count the total number correct for each child. Using the guidelines below, record the child's score on the Individual Record for the Unit 6 Benchmark Assessment (T72).

Number Correct	Rating	
8	Proficient	+
6 – 7	Developing	✓
Less than 6	Emerging	–

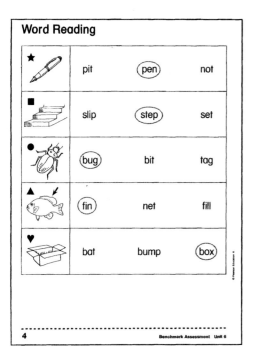

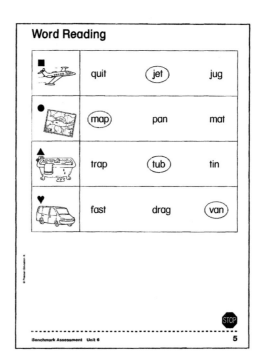

3. Word Knowledge: High-Frequency Words

(Individual or small group)

Purpose: Assesses ability to immediately recognize high-frequency words.

Hand out student pages 6–7. Children are to circle each word as you say it aloud. Move through the assessment quickly to make sure you are assessing the child's ability to recognize the high-frequency words quickly.

I am going to say one word in each row. You are going to circle the word I say. Find the first row with the square in it. Put your finger on it. Now look at the three words in that row. Draw a circle around the word *go . . . go.*

Move down to the next row. Put your finger on the circle. Look at the three words. Circle the word *said . . . said.*

Move down to the next row. Put your finger on the triangle. Look at the three words. Circle the word *come . . . come.*

Move down to the next row. Put your finger on the heart. Look at the three words. Circle the word *are . . . are.*

Move down to the next row. Put your finger on the rectangle. Look at the three words. Circle the word *two . . . two.*

Move down to the next row. Put your finger on the diamond. Look at the three words. Circle the word *five . . . five.*

Move down to the next row. Put your finger on the oval. Look at the three words. Circle the word *do . . . do.*

Go to the next page. Look at the top row with the square in it. Put your finger on the square. Look at the three words. Circle the word *green . . . green.*

Move down to the next row. Put your finger on the circle. Look at the three words. Circle the word *what . . . what.*

Move down to the next row, the last row. Put your finger on the triangle. Look at the three words. Circle the word *one . . . one.*

Scoring: For each child, count the total number of words circled correctly. Using the guidelines below, record the child's score on the Individual Record for the Unit 6 Benchmark Assessment (T72).

Number Correct	Rating	
10	Proficient	+
8 – 9	Developing	✓
Less than 8	Emerging	–

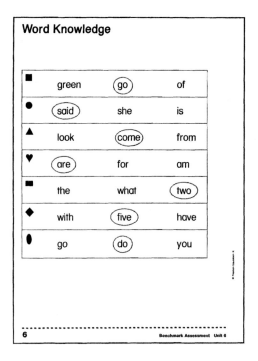

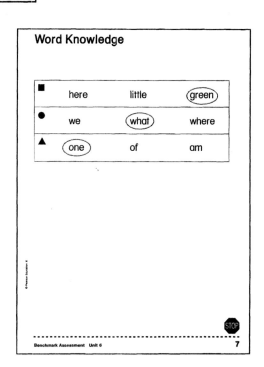

4. Listening Comprehension: Character, Setting, Plot

(Individual, small group, or whole class)

Purpose: Assesses general comprehension.

Hand out student page 8. Read aloud the introduction and the story printed in **bold.** Then read each question that follows. Children are to respond by circling the best answer to each question.

I am going to read a story about a cat named Maggie. Then I will ask you some questions. Listen carefully. Here is the story.

Maggie was an old cat who lived in a garden with birds and squirrels and snakes. She had a little house in the back of the yard. When it rained, Maggie would go into her little house in a corner of the garden and sit on her green pillow. From there she could watch the rain fall on the bushes and trees.

The family Maggie belonged to gave her two meals every day. One was breakfast, and the other was dinner. They put Maggie's bowl on the picnic table in the garden. In the morning, Maggie would eat only half her food. She would save the other half so that she could have snacks during the day. At dinnertime, she did the same thing. She would eat only half her food and save the rest to snack on at night.

The squirrels who lived in the garden enjoyed Maggie's snacks too. A squirrel would run to Maggie's bowl, take one piece of food, and scramble up a tree. Maggie did not mind sharing with the squirrels because they did not eat many snacks.

Then one day some sparrows began to snack on Maggie's food. The birds flew down from the tree and perched on Maggie's bowl. They pecked away at the food that was left in the bowl. Soon all Maggie's food was gone. This happened the next day too.

Maggie had a problem, but she knew what she had to do about it. She began to eat her breakfast slowly until she finished it all. She did the same thing with her dinner. She didn't leave any food for the sparrows to steal. She didn't have any food left for snacks, but she never felt hungry because she was very full from eating all her food at one time. The sparrows in the garden found out that an old cat can learn new tricks.

Now I am going to ask you some questions about the story. For each question there are three pictures. Draw a circle around the picture that shows the best answer. Listen carefully.

1. Look at the first row of pictures at the top of the page where you see the square. Put your finger on the square. What kind of animal is Maggie? Draw a circle around the picture that shows what kind of animal Maggie is.

2. Move down to the next row of pictures where you see the circle. Put your finger on the circle. Where did Maggie live? Circle the picture that shows where Maggie lived.

3. Move down to the next row of pictures where you see the triangle. Put your finger on the triangle. Where did Maggie go when it rained? Circle the picture that shows where Maggie went when it rained.

4. Move down to the next row of pictures where you see the heart. Put your finger on the heart. What animals ate all Maggie's food? Circle the picture that shows what animals ate all Maggie's food.

5. Move down to the last row of pictures where you see the rectangle. Put your finger on the rectangle. What did Maggie's food bowl look like at the end of the story? Circle the picture that shows what Maggie's food bowl looked like at the end of the story.

Scoring: For each child, mark the answer to each question correct or incorrect. Then count the total number correct for each child. Using the guidelines below, record the child's score on the Individual Record for the Unit 6 Benchmark Assessment (T72).

Number Correct	Rating	
5	Proficient	+
3 – 4	Developing	✓
Less than 3	Emerging	–

5. Writing: Sentences

(Individual, small group, or whole class)

Purpose: Assesses ability to write a sentence using an appropriate verb.

Hand out student page 9. Instruct children as follows.

Think about something you have learned about building things. Draw a picture about building something. Then write a sentence that tells what is happening in the picture. Remember that there should be a verb in your sentence.

Note: If children have trouble thinking of something to draw, remind them of some of the things they have learned about building things in the selections.

Scoring: Using the guidelines below, evaluate the child's work and record the child's score on the Individual Record for the Unit 6 Benchmark Assessment (T72).

Scoring Guidelines	Rating	
The picture shows something being built with some detail. The sentence contains a verb, tells about the picture, and is generally written correctly.	Proficient	+
The picture is recognizable. There is a sentence or part of a sentence that includes a verb, but the words may include a few errors.	Developing	✓
Attempts to draw a picture and write the sentence, but both are less than complete and correct.	Emerging	−

Writing

Benchmark Assessment Unit 6   9

INDIVIDUAL RECORD

Unit 6 Benchmark Assessment

Child's Name _____ **Date** _____

Directions: Record the results of the Unit 6 Benchmark Assessment by marking Proficient (+), Developing (✓), or Emerging (–) beside each assessed skill.

Unit 6 Assessed Skills	Proficient (+)	Developing (✓)	Emerging (–)
Phonemic Awareness: Blend Individual Phonemes			
Word Reading: CVC, CVCC, CCVC words			
Word Knowledge: High-Frequency Words			
Listening Comprehension: Character, Setting, Plot			
Writing: Sentence with an appropriate verb			

Notes/Observations

Benchmark Assessment Teacher's Manual

CLASS RECORD CHART

Skills Assessment   Unit _____

Teacher's Name _____ Date _____

Directions: Use this chart to record the results for all children on any of the Unit Benchmark Assessments. Fill in the number of the unit at the top. Beside each child's name, record the results of the Unit Benchmark Assessment by marking Proficient (+), Developing (✓), Emerging (–) beside each assessed skill.

Child's Name	Phonemic Awareness	Phonological Awareness	Letter Naming	Phonics	Word Knowledge	Word Reading	Comprehension	Writing
1.								
2.								
3.								
4.								
5.								
6.								
7.								
8.								
9.								
10.								
11.								
12.								
13.								
14.								
15.								
16.								
17.								
18.								
19.								
20.								
21.								
22.								
23.								
24.								

NAME _____ DATE _____

Scott Foresman
Benchmark Assessment
Unit 1
All Together Now

Editorial Offices: Glenview, Illinois • Parsippany, New Jersey
New York, New York
Sales Offices: Boston, Massachusetts • Duluth, Georgia • Glenview, Illinois
Coppell, Texas • Sacramento, California • Mesa, Arizona

11 12 13 14 15 16 17 18 19 20 V036 15 14 13 12 11 10

ISBN 0-328-19572-3

90000

9 780328 195725

Letter Naming

M	r	T	u	p	R	P	f	A
S	G	b	E	K	o	w	n	Z
y	a	W	N	L	e	d	h	s
V	q	O	i	z	U	g	m	v
D	c	X	J	F	Q	j	x	C
H	k	B	l	Y	I	t		

STOP

Phonological Awareness

Word Knowledge

am

the

I

little

to

a

Listening Comprehension

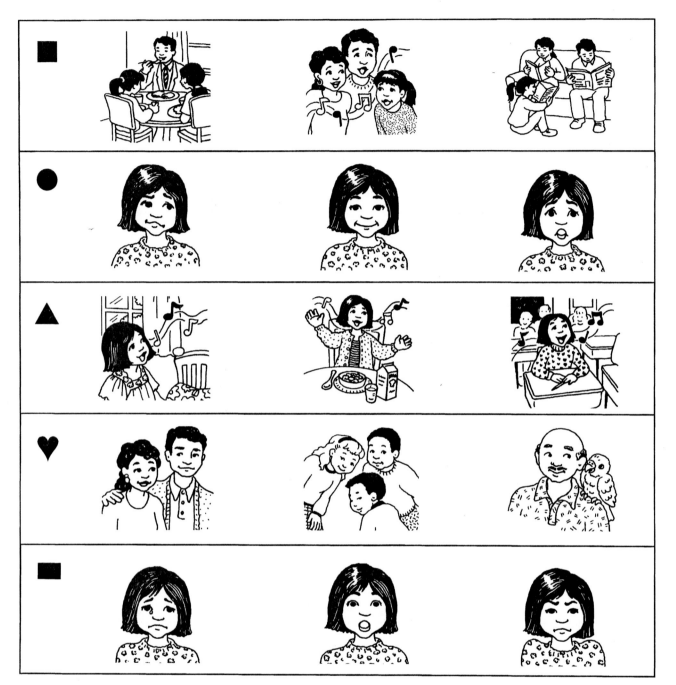

Writing

Attributes

Picture: _____ eyes   _____ nose   _____ mouth   _____ hair

_____ neck   _____ body   _____ clothes   _____ arms

_____ hands   _____ legs   _____ feet

Name: _____ all letters are present   _____ all letters are written correctly

_____ first letter is capitalized

STOP

NAME _____ DATE _____

Scott Foresman
Benchmark Assessment
Unit 2
Animals Live Here

Editorial Offices: Glenview, Illinois • Parsippany, New Jersey
New York, New York
Sales Offices: Boston, Massachusetts • Duluth, Georgia • Glenview, Illinois
Coppell, Texas • Sacramento, California • Mesa, Arizona

Copyright © Pearson Education, Inc.

11 12 13 14 15 16 17 18 19 20 V036 15 14 13 12 11 10

ISBN 0-328-19573-1

90000

Phonemic Awareness

Phonemic Awareness

■		
●		
▲		

STOP

Phonics

★	a u i
■	m b r
●	s t f
▲	e a o
♥	s n d

Phonics

■ (pan)	t k p
● (car)	f s c
▲ (fish)	i e u

STOP

Word Knowledge

★	have	am	the
■	a	like	is
●	we	I	am
▲	he	my	we
♥	the	little	like
▬	he	me	we
◆	little	for	to

Comprehension

STOP

Writing

NAME _____ DATE _____

Scott Foresman
Benchmark Assessment
Unit 3
Watch Me Change

Editorial Offices: Glenview, Illinois • Parsippany, New Jersey
New York, New York
Sales Offices: Boston, Massachusetts • Duluth, Georgia • Glenview, Illinois
Coppell, Texas • Sacramento, California • Mesa, Arizona

ISBN 0-328-19574-X

11 12 13 14 15 16 17 18 19 20 V036 15 14 13 12 11 10

Phonemic Awareness

Phonemic Awareness

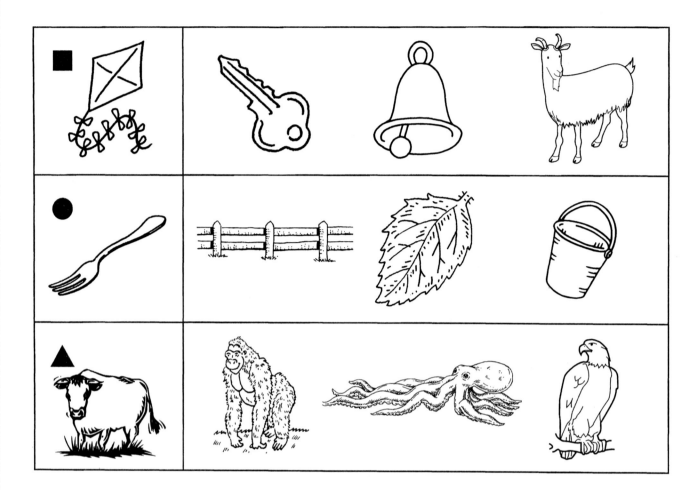

STOP

Benchmark Assessment   Unit 3

Phonics

★ (mat image)	m c r
■ (bed image)	b t k
● (nail image)	s d n
▲ (rabbit image)	c s r
♥ (dog image)	f d p

Phonics

■	t k g
●	f h j
▲	u i o

STOP

Word Knowledge

★	am	me	the
■	with	mat	we
●	she	sit	he
▲	little	look	ball
♥	cat	sun	see
▬	have	met	they
◆	you	my	yes
⬭	a	of	for

© Pearson Education K

Comprehension

STOP

Writing

NAME _____ DATE _____

Scott Foresman
Benchmark Assessment
Unit 4
Let's Explore

Reading STREET
Grade K

PEARSON

Scott
Foresman

Editorial Offices: Glenview, Illinois • Parsippany, New Jersey
New York, New York
Sales Offices: Boston, Massachusetts • Duluth, Georgia • Glenview, Illinois
Coppell, Texas • Sacramento, California • Mesa, Arizona

ISBN 0-328-19575-8

11 12 13 14 15 16 17 18 19 20 V036 15 14 13 12 11 10

90000
9 780328 195756

Phonemic Awareness

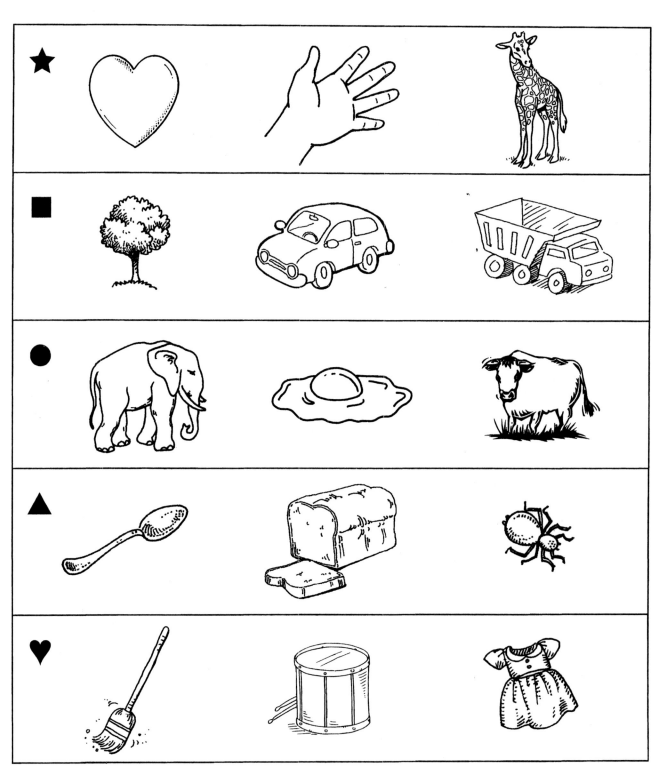

Phonemic Awareness

STOP

- - - - **Phonemic Awareness** -

Phonics

★	dr	bl	tr
■	st	sp	dr
●	bl	dr	br
▲	h	l	g
♥	a	e	o

Phonics

■	r s h
●	f l g
▲	sp st lk
♥	st lk sp

STOP

Word Reading

★ [cat image]	cat	cot	cap
■ [bed image]	bat	bet	bed
● [hat image]	hat	ham	hit
▲ [net image]	tan	net	not
♥ [top image]	top	dot	pet
■ [safety pin image]	pot	pig	pin

STOP

- - - Word Reading -

Word Knowledge

★	am	are	red
■	mat	the	that
●	do	you	to
▲	one	not	go
♥	they	you	two
▬	we	three	the
◆	fan	of	four
⬮	five	like	have

© Pearson Education K

Word Knowledge

■	we	here	he
●	get	he	go
▲	for	from	my

© Pearson Education **K**

Word Knowledge

Benchmark Assessment   Unit 4

Comprehension

STOP

Writing

STOP

NAME _____ DATE _____

Scott Foresman
Benchmark Assessment
Unit 5
Going Places

PEARSON
Scott Foresman

Editorial Offices: Glenview, Illinois • Parsippany, New Jersey
New York, New York
Sales Offices: Boston, Massachusetts • Duluth, Georgia • Glenview, Illinois
Coppell, Texas • Sacramento, California • Mesa, Arizona

11 12 13 14 15 16 17 18 19 20 V036 15 14 13 12 11 10

ISBN 0-328-19576-6

9 780328 195763

90000

Phonemic Awareness

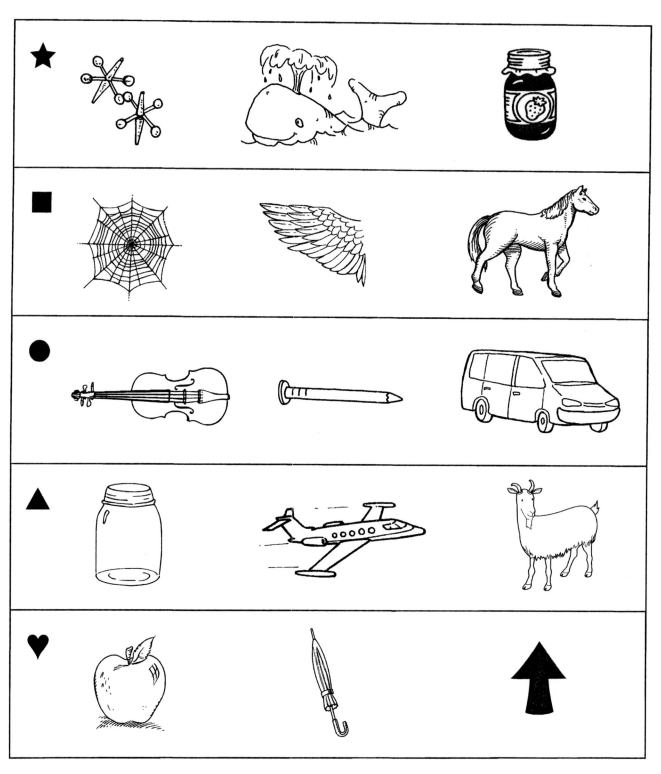

Phonemic Awareness

STOP

Phonics

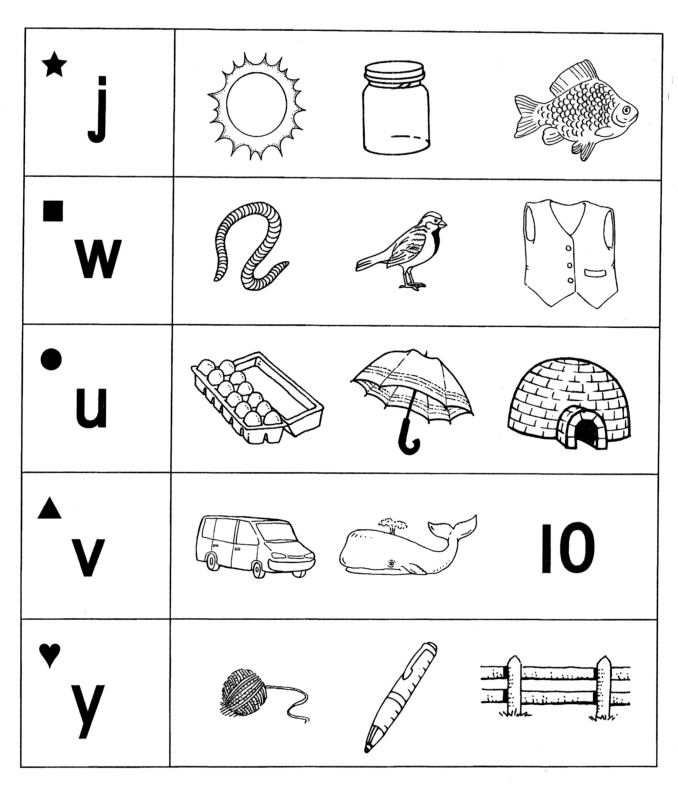

Phonics

STOP

Word Reading

★	can	pet	cup
■	pin	nap	big
●	bat	pat	bag
▲ 10	net	ten	top
♥	dot	bed	box

© Pearson Education K

Word Reading

■ (log image)	dog	log	led
● (man image)	man	mud	mop
▲ (sun image)	sat	sun	ran
♥ (bib image)	bad	bud	bib

STOP

Word Knowledge

■	yellow	yes	you
●	go	ten	green
▲	blue	look	you
♥	with	we	what
▬	have	said	see
◆	was	what	one
⬮	here	they	where
⬢	can	come	my

Comprehension

STOP

Writing

STOP

© Pearson Education **K**

NAME _____ DATE _____

Scott Foresman
Benchmark Assessment
Unit 6
Building Our Homes

Editorial Offices: Glenview, Illinois • Parsippany, New Jersey
New York, New York
Sales Offices: Boston, Massachusetts • Duluth, Georgia • Glenview, Illinois
Coppell, Texas • Sacramento, California • Mesa, Arizona

ISBN 0-328-19577-4

11 12 13 14 15 16 17 18 19 20 V036 15 14 13 12 11 10

Phonemic Awareness

Phonemic Awareness

STOP

Phonemic Awareness

Benchmark Assessment   Unit 6

Word Reading

★	pit pen not	
■	slip step set	
●	bug bit tag	
▲	fin net fill	
♥	bat bump box	

Word Reading

■	quit	jet	jug
●	map	pan	mat
▲	trap	tub	tin
♥	fast	drag	van

STOP

Word Knowledge

■	green	go	of
●	said	she	is
▲	look	come	from
♥	are	for	am
▬	the	what	two
◆	with	five	have
⬤	go	do	you

- -

Word Knowledge

■	here	little	green
●	we	what	where
▲	one	of	am

STOP

Comprehension

© Pearson Education K

Writing